Turn Your Chaos *Into Calm*

Bruno the Poodle's Quotes and Prompts to Reveal New Paths to Balance

BOOK I

J. J. Jordan

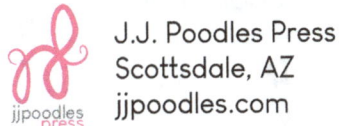

J.J. Poodles Press
Scottsdale, AZ
jjpoodles.com

Turn Your Chaos Into Calm, Book I of the Lifestyle Journal Series

Published by

J.J. Poodles Press
Scottsdale, AZ
jjpoodles.com

Copyright ©2021 J.J. Jordan. All rights reserved.

No part of this book may be reproduced or transmitted in any form or by any means, electronic or mechanical, including photocopying, recording, or by any information storage and retrieval system, without permission in writing from the copyright owner.

Scripture quotations marked (TLB) are taken from The Living Bible copyright © 1971. Used by permission of Tyndale House Publishers, Inc., Carol Stream, Illinois 60188. All rights reserved.

Scripture quotations marked TPT are from The Passion Translation®. Copyright © 2017, 2018 by Passion & Fire Ministries, Inc. Used by permission. All rights reserved. thePassionTranslation.com.

This book was printed in the United States of America.

Cover Design by Angie Alaya of pro_ebookcovers

Interior Design by DocUmeantDesigns
www.DocUmeantDesigns.com

ISBN: 978-1-7340944-2-8

Contents

V   INTRODUCTION

1   PART 1: FRIENDS & RELATIONSHIPS

51   PART 2: SPIRITUALITY, HOPE, & MEANING

79   PART 3: HEALTH, NUTRITION, & EXERCISE

105   PART 4: CAREER

Introduction

2020. Ugh! One of the toughest, most unprecedented years in current history. A world-wide health crisis. Civil unrest. A divisive competition for the U.S. presidency. Even wild weather patterns.

As I watched the chaos in the world unfolding, and experienced its turbulent fallout in my immediate circle, I yearned for calm. I spoke with friends and family and found most searching for solace as well. And we are not alone. Many others, probably including you, reel with imbalance and are seeking for ways to cope.

This realization prompted me to create this book to serve you as a beautiful quiet eye in the hurricane of present-day life. Its inspirational quotes can help bring you back into balance and focus, no matter what happens to you or around you. It also provides areas to write down your goals, visions, and action items. Journaling—therapeutic in itself—can spark enlightened thoughts. These bring clarity and fresh ideas to create more harmony and joy in your experience. The more you do it, the easier it becomes, and the more the ideas flow.

I designed the book to provide inspiration, so don't feel like you need to use it from cover to cover. Pick and choose an area/topic to write about every day, or as the mood hits you. I encourage you to be patient with your progress, and to celebrate even the smallest accomplishment as you mindfully wind your way through the raging storm toward inner peace.

This first book will touch on the important topics of friends, relationships, spirituality, hope and meaning, health, nutrition, exercise, and career. At the beginning of each section is a Balance Wheel specific to the chapter. Think of your life as wheels. Are your wheels well-rounded and balanced? You can pick a section of the wheel that may need maintenance. Just like the wheels on your car need to be balanced and aligned, so does your life. This Journal will help you keep your life calm, chaos free, and in balance.

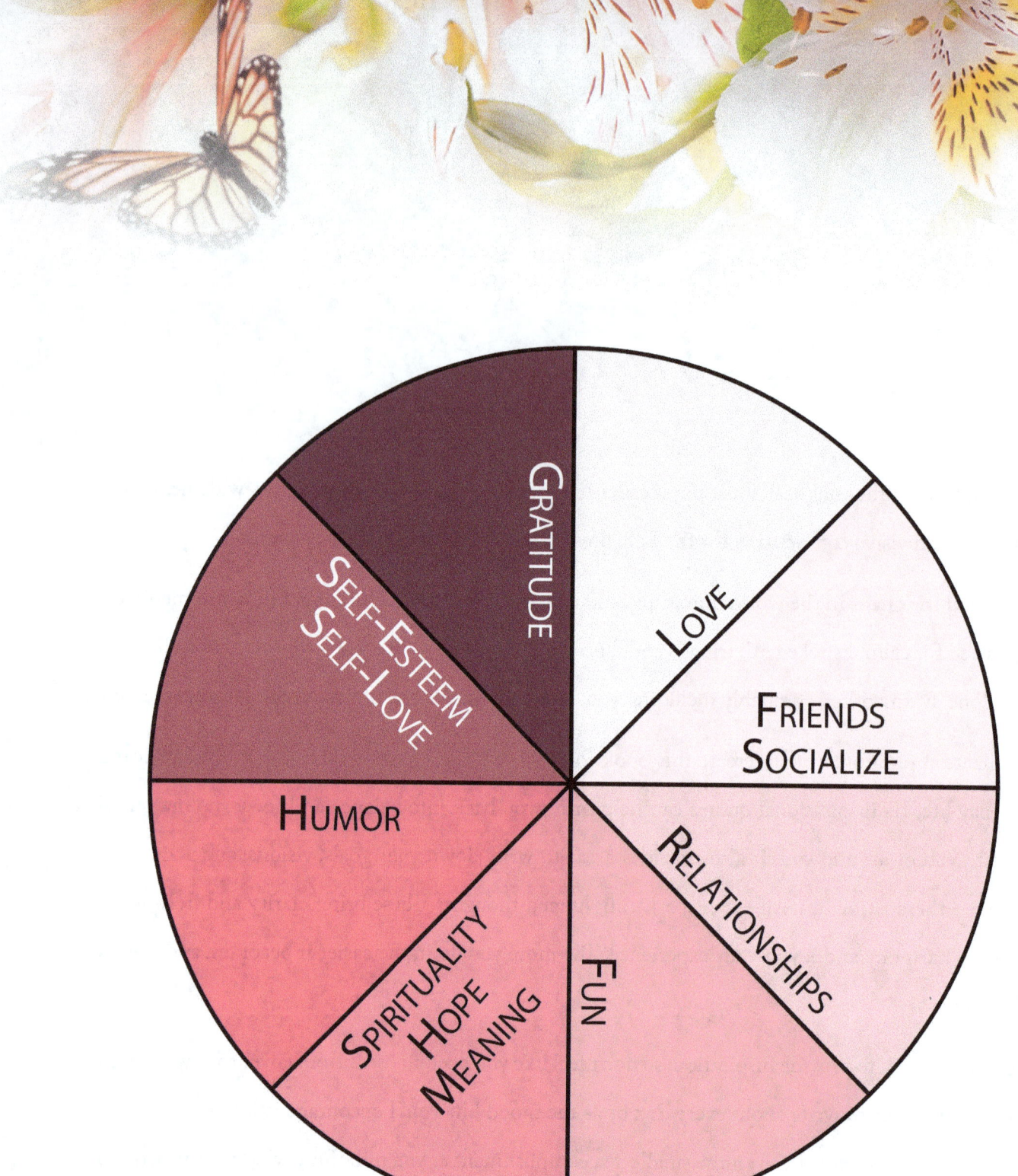

Part 1
Friends & Relationships

Memory is the diary that we all carry about us. —Oscar Wilde

What defining memories do you remember regarding friendships and relationships?

Action Plan & Goals

Regarding Friends & Relationships—Stay in **Balance & Live Fully**.

I commit to:

"Always forgive your enemy, nothing annoys them so much." —Anonymous

Do you forgive others? If not, why not? How does it serve you to forgive or not forgive?

Action Plan & Goals

Regarding Friends & Relationships—Stay in **Balance & Live Fully**.

I commit to: _____

_____

_____

"The world has grown suspicious of anything that looks like a happily married life." —Oscar Wilde

How many married couples do you know and what do you find you would like to mirror in your own close relationships?

Action Plan & Goals

Regarding Friends & Relationships—Stay in **Balance & Live Fully**.

I commit to:

"True friends stab you in the front." —Oscar Wilde

Do you allow friends to be honest and frank with you, even if it hurts?

Action Plan & Goals

Regarding Friends & Relationships—Stay in **Balance & Live Fully.**

I commit to:

"Friends that make you laugh until you cry are worth keeping in touch with very often." — J.J. Jordan

Who have you lost touch with that makes you laugh until you cry? List who you want to touch base with soon.

Action Plan & Goals

Regarding Friends & Relationships—Stay in **Balance & Live Fully**.

I commit to:

"Rudeness is the weak man's version of strength."—Anonymous

Are you nice, kind and respectful to all mankind? Where or when have you encountered rude and disrespectful people? How can you be nice and respectful today?

Action Plan & Goals

Regarding Friends & Relationships—Stay in **Balance & Live Fully**.

I commit to:

"The weak can never forgive; forgiveness is the attribute of the strong." —Gandi 1869–1948

Do you forgive? How can you be strong and have forgiveness for those that have harmed you?

Action Plan & Goals

Regarding Friends & Relationships—Stay in **Balance & Live Fully**.

I commit to:

"In the end, people appreciate frankness more than flattery" (Proverbs 28:23 TLB).

Are you frank, honest and genuine with others?

Action Plan & Goals

Regarding Friends & Relationships—Stay in **Balance & Live Fully**.

I commit to:

"If you try to get rid of fear and anger without knowing their meaning; they will grow stronger and return."
— Deepak Chopra

Do you know the meaning behind your fear and anger? How can you release fear and anger now?

Action Plan & Goals

Regarding Friends & Relationships—Stay in **Balance & Live Fully**.

I commit to:

"The best and most beautiful things in the world cannot be seen or even touched. They must be felt with the heart."
— Helen Keller

What friends and relationships touch your heart and in what way?

Action Plan & Goals

Regarding Friends & Relationships—Stay in **Balance & Live Fully**.

I commit to:

"A good friend is like a four leaf clover; hard to find and lucky to have." —Irish Proverb

Make a list of your friends who are like four leaf clovers to you. Who do you need to keep in touch with soon?

Action Plan & Goals

Regarding Friends & Relationships—Stay in **Balance & Live Fully**.

I commit to:

"Friendship is the only cement that will ever hold the world together." —Woodrow T. Wilson

Are you needing more friends in your life? Make a list of where and how you can make new connections with like-minded friends.

Action Plan & Goals

Regarding Friends & Relationships—Stay in **Balance & Live Fully**.

I commit to:

"A sweet friendship refreshes the soul" (Proverbs 27:9 TPT).

How can you be sweet to your friends? Do you have any sweet or sour friends?

Action Plan & Goals

Regarding Friends & Relationships—Stay in **Balance & Live Fully**.

I commit to:

"Rudeness is the weak man's imitation of strength." —Eric Hoffer 1902–1983

Are you willing to let go of Rude people in your life, if not why not?

Action Plan & Goals

Regarding Friends & Relationships—Stay in **Balance & Live Fully**.

I commit to:

Being happy-go-lucky around a person whose heart is heavy, is as bad as stealing his jacket in cold weather or rubbing salt in his wounds" (Proverbs 25:20 TLB).

Are you or are others compassionate towards your circumstances? If so, how?

_____
_____
_____
_____
_____
_____
_____
_____
_____
_____
_____
_____
_____
_____
_____
_____
_____
_____
_____

Action Plan & Goals

Regarding Friends & Relationships—Stay in **Balance & Live Fully**.

I commit to:

"Keep away from people who try to belittle your ambitions. Small people always do that, but the really great make you feel that you, too, can become great." —Mark Twain

Are your relationships encouraging or discouraging?

Action Plan & Goals

Regarding Friends & Relationships—Stay in **Balance & Live Fully**.

I commit to:

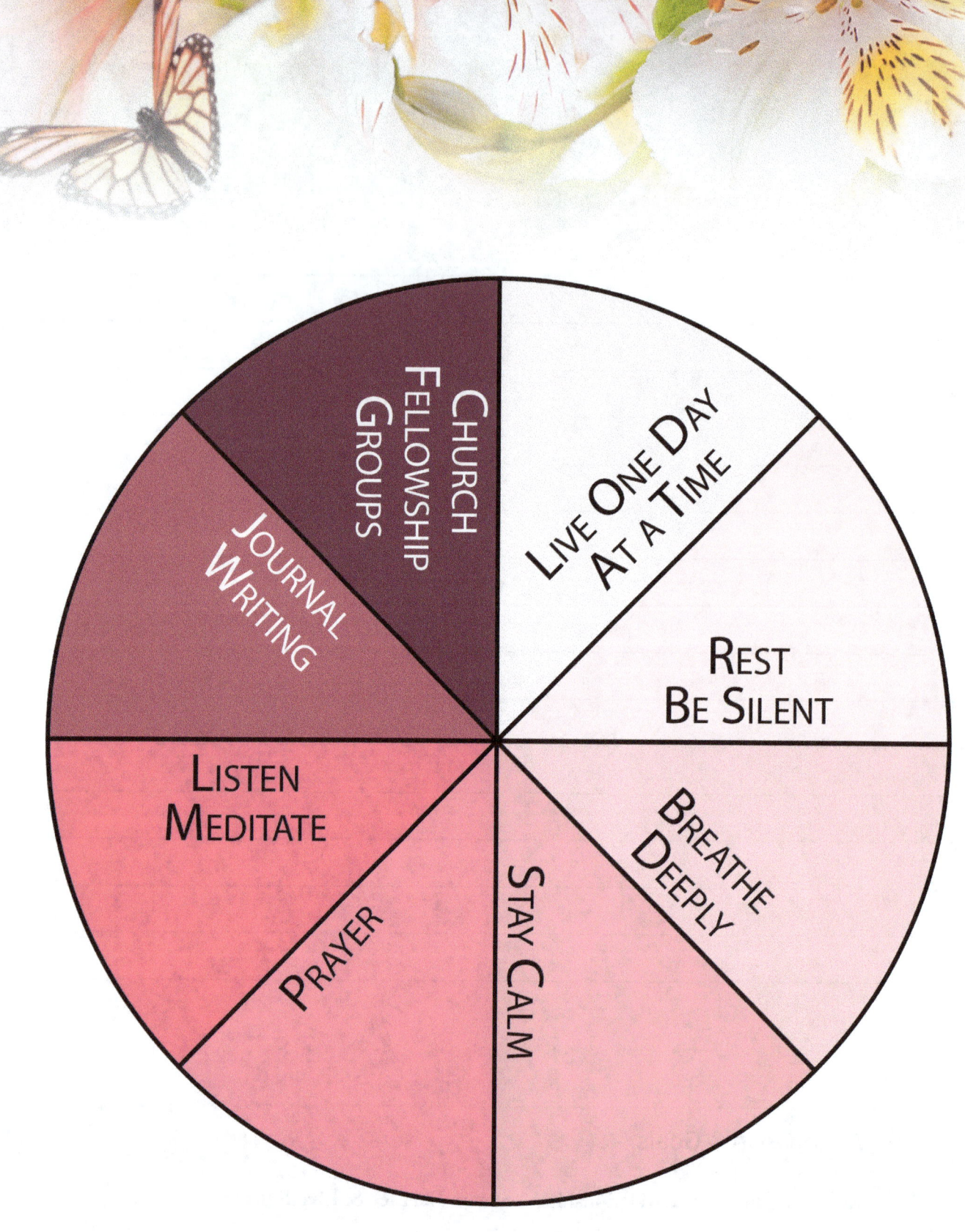

The Author, The Star and the Keeper is a (must see) film of 2020!
Salty Earth Pictures By President Steven Zambo
saltyearthpictures.org

Part 2
Spirituality, Hope, & Meaning

"What you dismiss as an ordinary coincidence may be an opening to an extraordinary advantage." — Deepak Chopra

What coincidences have happened to you this week, month or year that has given you meaning and hope?

....
....
....
....
....
....
....
....
....
....
....
....

Action Plan & Goals

Regarding Spirituality, Hope, & Meaning to stay in **Balance & Live Fully**.

I commit to:

"Only a life lived for others is a life worthwhile." —Albert Einstein

How have you been of service to others that makes your life worthwhile and gives your life meaning?

Action Plan & Goals

Regarding Spirituality, Hope, & Meaning to stay in **Balance & Live Fully**.

I commit to:

"Coincidence is God's way of remaining anonymous." —Albert Einstein

What coincidences have happened in your life this week, month or year?

Action Plan & Goals

Regarding Spirituality, Hope, & Meaning to stay in **Balance & Live Fully**.

I commit to:

"I attract miracles effortlessly and safely." —J. J. Jordan

What miracles have happened in your life?

Action Plan & Goals

Regarding Spirituality, Hope, & Meaning to stay in **Balance & Live Fully**.

I commit to:

"What ever happens around you, don't take it personally. Nothing other people do is because of you. It is because of themselves." —Don Miguel Ruiz, *The Four Agreements*

Are you taking other people's behaviors personally? If so, why?

Action Plan & Goals

Regarding Spirituality, Hope, & Meaning to stay in **Balance & Live Fully**.

I commit to:

"I want you to forget everything you have learned in your whole life. This is the beginning of a new understanding, a new dream." —Don Miguel Ruiz, *The Four Agreements*

What or how can you create a new life; a new vision and dream for your life? Can you now unlearn what is no longer true and is no longer serving you?

_____

_____

_____

_____

_____

_____

_____

_____

_____

_____

_____

_____

_____

_____

_____

_____

_____

_____

Action Plan & Goals

Regarding Spirituality, Hope, & Meaning to stay in **Balance & Live Fully**.

I commit to:

"Feelings come and go like clouds in a windy sky. Conscious breathing is my anchor." —Thich Nhat Hahn

Are you remembering to practice meditation? Do you practice breathing exercises?

Action Plan & Goals

Regarding Spirituality, Hope, & Meaning to stay in **Balance & Live Fully**.

I commit to:

"Get yourself grounded and you can navigate even the stormiest roads in peace." —Steve Goodier

Do you believe that the Greater your storm, the brighter your rainbow will be?

Action Plan & Goals

Regarding Spirituality, Hope, & Meaning to stay in **Balance & Live Fully**.

I commit to:

"Flying starts from the ground. The more grounded you are the higher you can fly." —J. R. Rim

Are you grounded in the now?

Action Plan & Goals

Regarding Spirituality, Hope, & Meaning to stay in **Balance & Live Fully**.

I commit to: _____

_____

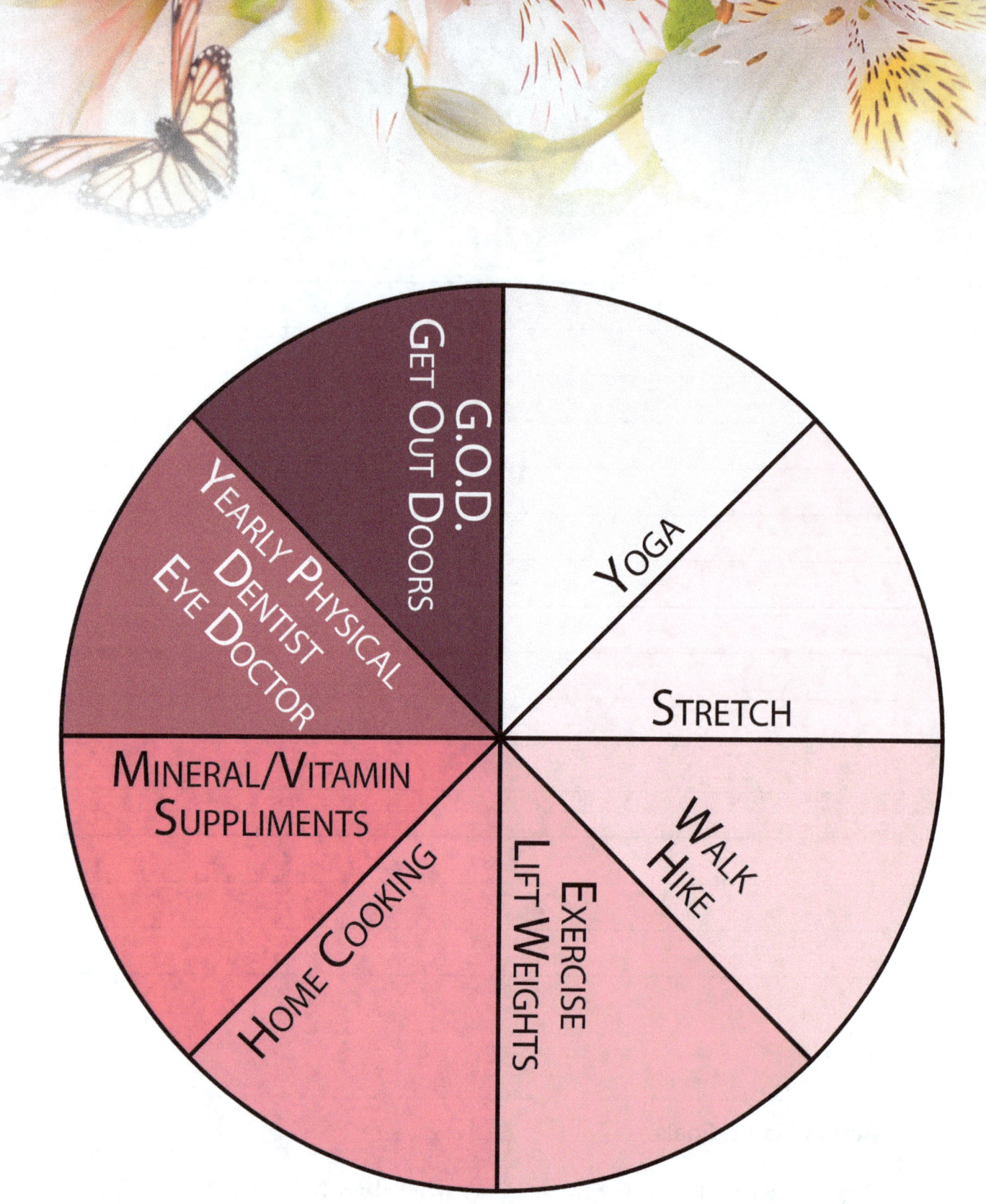

The ORGANIC RED SUPREMEFOOD® & FERMENTED GREEN SUPREMEFOOD® carried by Divine Health and formulated by Don Colbert, M.D. are wonderful supplements to take daily.
divinehealth.com

Part 3
Health, Nutrition, & Exercise

"There is no love sincerer than the love of food." —Anonymous

What foods do you love that you would like to make soon?

....
....
....
....
....
....
....
....
....
....
....
....

Action Plan & Goals

Regarding Health, Nutrition, & Exercise to stay in **Balance & Live Fully**.

I commit to:

"Nature has given us all the pieces required to achieve exceptional wellness and health; but has left it to us to put these pieces together." —Drane McLaren

What can you add to your grocery list to maintain a healthy diet?

Action Plan & Goals

Regarding Health, Nutrition, & Exercise to stay in **Balance & Live Fully**.

I commit to:

"Insanity: Doing the same thing over and over again and expecting different results." —Albert Einstein

Are you willing to change your diet and what you are eating?

Action Plan & Goals

Regarding Health, Nutrition, & Exercise to stay in **Balance & Live Fully**.

I commit to:

"By choosing healthy over skinny, you are choosing self-love over self-judgement." —Steve Maraboli

Are you accepting your body as it is, whole and perfect, no matter what size it is?

Action Plan & Goals

Regarding Health, Nutrition, & Exercise to stay in **Balance & Live Fully**.

I commit to:

"Take care of your body. It's the only place you have to live." —Jim Rohn

What are you doing to take care of your body today?

Action Plan & Goals

Regarding Health, Nutrition, & Exercise to stay in **Balance & Live Fully**.

I commit to:

"A journey of a thousand miles begins with a single step." —Lao Tzu

What steps are you taking today to get more exercise today or this week?

Action Plan & Goals

Regarding Health, Nutrition, & Exercise to stay in **Balance & Live Fully**.

I commit to:

"Get comfortable with being uncomfortable." —Jillian Michaels

Are you willing to be uncomfortable and get moving?

Action Plan & Goals

Regarding Health, Nutrition, & Exercise to stay in **Balance & Live Fully**.

I commit to:

"If you are in a bad mood go for a walk. If you are still in a bad mood go for another walk." —Hippocrates

Have you been walking enough to shake off a bad mood?

Action Plan & Goals

Regarding Health, Nutrition, & Exercise to stay in **Balance & Live Fully**.

I commit to:

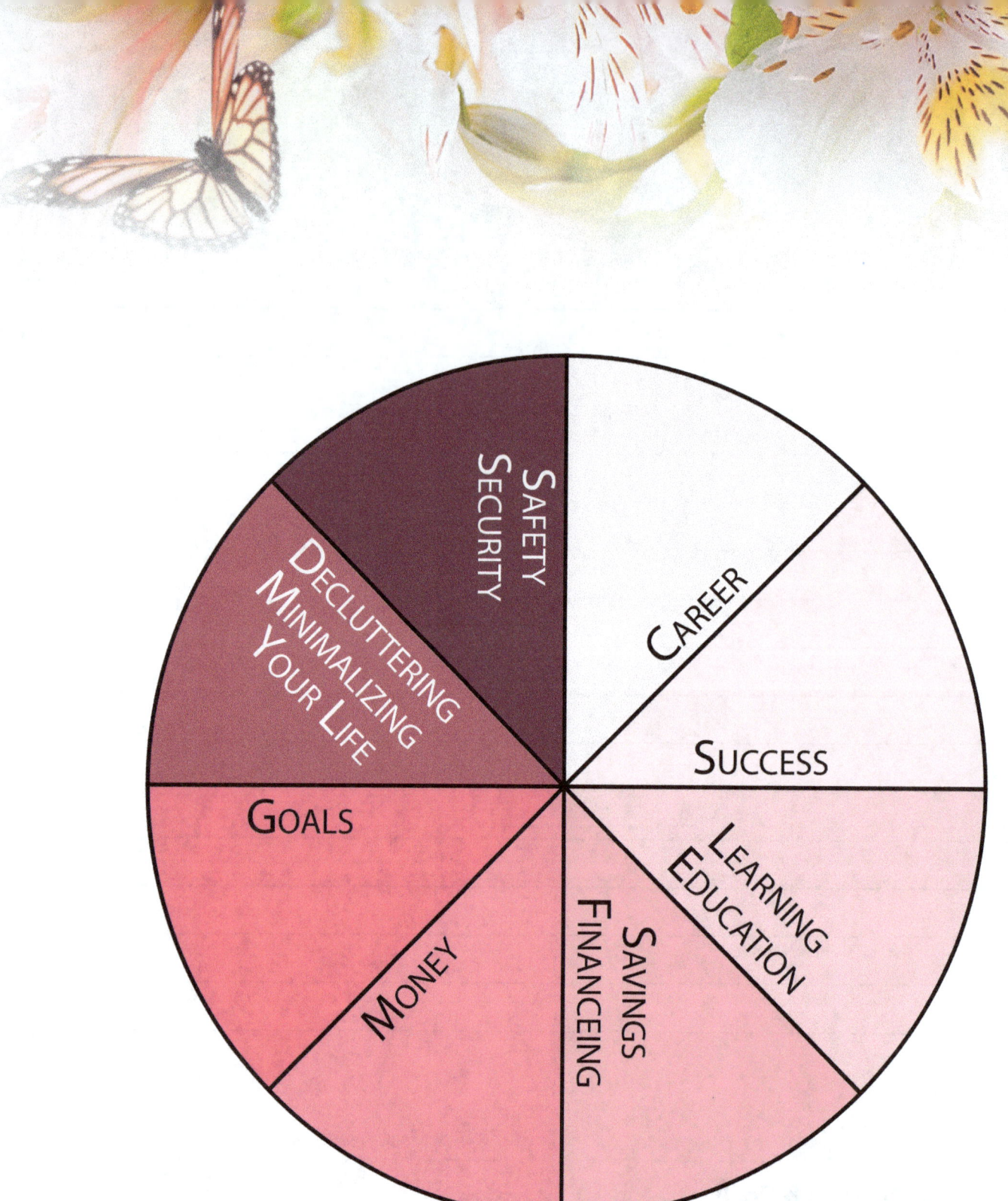

Part 4
Career

"The beginning is the most important part of the work." —Plato

What steps can you start or take to begin a new career?

_____
_____
_____
_____
_____
_____
_____
_____
_____
_____
_____
_____
_____
_____

Action Plan & Goals

Regarding moving towards a new Career. Stay in **Balance & Live Fully**.

I commit to:

"When you change your thoughts remember to also change your world." —Norman Vincent Peale

What thoughts have you changed to help you find a new career?

Action Plan & Goals

Regarding moving towards a new Career. Stay in **Balance & Live Fully**.

I commit to:

"You can do anything you set your mind to do." —Benjamin Franklin

What are you set in your mind to do?

Action Plan & Goals

Regarding moving towards a new Career. Stay in **Balance & Live Fully**.

I commit to:

"Look. Before, or you'll find yourself behind." —Benjamin Franklin

Do you have a plan to look forward towards a bright future? Are you living in the past?

Action Plan & Goals

Regarding moving towards a new Career. Stay in **Balance & Live Fully**.

I commit to:

"Well done is better than well said." —Benjamin Franklin

Are you just talking about what you want to do? What steps are you taking instead of just talking about it?

Action Plan & Goals

Regarding moving towards a new Career. Stay in **Balance & Live Fully**.

I commit to:

"I didn't get there by wishing for it or hoping for it; but by working for it." —Estee Lauder

What are you willing to work for instead of just hoping to change?

Part 4 Career | 121

Action Plan & Goals

Regarding moving towards a new Career. Stay in **Balance & Live Fully**.

I commit to:

www.ingramcontent.com/pod-product-compliance
Lightning Source LLC
Chambersburg PA
CBHW081115080526
44587CB00021B/3599